THE STORY OF
HULL

by

Alan Avery

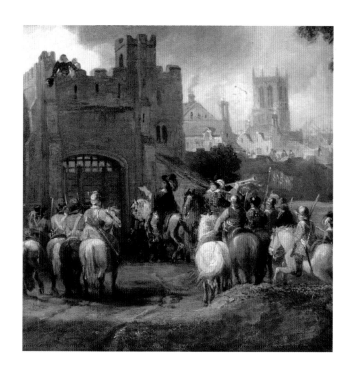

BLACKTHORN PRESS

Blackthorn Press, Blackthorn House
Middleton Rd, Pickering YO18 8AL
United Kingdom

ISBN 978 1 906259 03 7

© Alan Avery 2008

www.blackthornpress.com

Book design by Simon Ellis
Email: simon@flexibubbleart.co.uk

CONTENTS

THIS STATUE
was Erected in the
MDCCXXXI
To the Memo
KING WILLIA
OUR GREAT DEL

SURVEYORS

OF FINE ALE

THE BEGINNINGS OF HULL

Although the area surrounding the present day city of Hull is rich in prehistoric finds and the history of Roman and Anglo-Saxon and Viking East Yorkshire is well documented, the early history of Hull is unclear. The name Hull is probably of Danish origin meaning a deep cut. At the point where the River Hull enters the River Humber a natural harbour is formed, the Haven, and it is highly likely that it was used by local traders, seamen and invaders for that purpose, especially as it then gave access to inland East Yorkshire and the rich markets of Beverley and York.

Left
The Haven, where Hull now stands, was a place to load and unload cargo

But whether there was any permanent settlement on the site, we do not know. The area suffered then, as it does now, from flooding, as much of the surrounding land is below sea level and high tides and erosion would have made any settlement precarious. Even the course of the River Hull was not permanent, as it was known to have changed its course during the disastrous floods of 1253.

The Doomsday Book of 1086, when the new king, William I, sent out commissioners to record who owned what land and what there was on it, makes no mention of any buildings but it is likely that the area round the mouth of the River Hull was used as a loading point by local merchants. The Archbishop of York had rights to levy tolls and was in constant dispute with the monks of Meaux who owned the land and with the merchants who had to pay the tolls.

HULL IN THE MIDDLE AGES

The early history of Hull is closely linked with the Cistercian Abbey of Meaux, which was located near Beverley some ten miles north of Hull. The Abbey was founded in 1151 by William le Gros, the fourth Lord of Holderness and quickly grew in wealth as it was granted land by neighbouring barons and gentry hoping to gain favours for the 'next life'. In 1193 Mathilda Camin sold to the Abbey land 'of Wyc of Mitune' for eighty-seven marks of silver. Wyke in the manor of Myton, as it became known, is called a 'Vill' in the deed of sale, which would indicate that a small settlement had been established before the purchase in 1193. Wyke is a Danish name but where the first villagers came from is not clear. Wyke clustered around the river Hull while the manor of Myton spread further west perhaps as far as modern Spring Bank. There was a chapel in Myton by 1200 and another chapel, built by James Helward around 1230, was erected on the site of the present Holy Trinity church.

Right
A Hull Merchant
bargains for wool

The monks of Meaux derived most of their wealth from the wool trade and owned vast flocks of sheep on their land in Holderness. It is estimated that by 1394 they owned 20,000 acres of land. Much of the wool was exported to Flanders and Italy by merchants who would travel the country buying fleeces from the Abbeys and Monasteries. The sheep were sheared with hand-clippers and the fleeces crammed into canvas bags and sent by packhorse to the nearest port where the bags were weighed by the customs officer, a fee taken and then stamped with his mark. Once the wool had reached the foreign ports, the merchants would sell it to the spinners and weavers and then use the profits to buy luxury goods such as fine cloth and wine to bring back to England. Vast sums of money were made and many of the merchants were wealthy and powerful men. The revenue raised by the King through the fees charged at the customs houses were an important part of the royal income.

It is likely then, that the monks of Meaux were looking for a port close to their land where they could take part in this trade. Certainly they were active buying up land around the little settlement and cutting channels and enlarging streams that ran into the River Hull so that their wool could be transported by boat. They built themselves a hall on the site of the present Railway Dock and we can assume carried out work on the river bank to make it suitable for shipping.

One of the earliest streets we can identify is the present High Street, which runs alongside the River Hull and was then known as Hull Street. This eventually joined Monkgate where the monks built a court house during the 13th Century. This would indicate that the town was growing as more local merchants and tradesmen rented land from the monks and built themselves houses and warehouses to carry on their trades. The Box family traded in wine and rented land near Scale Lane where they built a quay for their ships. The Camin family were wealthy enough to be buying land in the town by the middle of the 12th century. By 1203 Hull was the sixth busiest port of England after London, Boston, Southampton, Lincoln and Lynn. In 1299 Hull merchants were trading with all of Europe from Norway to Greece, importing timber, olive oil, wine, furs and even oranges and lemons in exchange for wool, hides, lead, tin, coal and cheese.

The growing importance of the town was indicated in 1278 when the Abbot of Meaux petitioned King Edward I to be allowed to hold a weekly market and an annual fair. This was granted and by 1293 there was a market on Tuesdays and Fridays and a yearly fair. The markets brought local produce in from the surrounding countryside to feed the growing population in return for cash or for such goods as were manufactured in the town. The annual fair would attract merchants from all over Europe to barter and trade and to strike deals with the Hull merchants and ship owners.

Right
A Hull Merchant

Above Hull Market
began in 1293

The reign of Edward I (1272 – 1307) was an important one for many northern towns. The king had ambitions in Scotland and virtually moved the capital to York to be nearer the border. He needed a port which was safe from any possible attack from Scotland and yet accessible from the North Sea. The town of Wyke-upon-Hull fitted these purposes ideally and the King, who was in East Yorkshire in 1292, set about acquiring the village and neighbouring Myton from the monks of Meaux. No sum of money is mentioned as having changed hands, merely "great profit whereof we are well content". The documents which relate to the purchase in 1293 made an inventory of everything the King was acquiring and from them we can deduce that Wyke

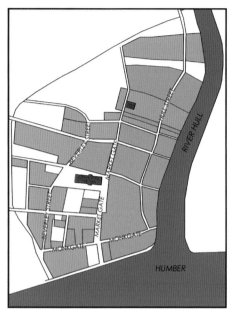

Left Hull in 1293

had a population of around 300. There were forty tenants, among them Geoffrey de Hotham and Walter le Celererman and even a few plots held by villeins still farming the land. A defensive ditch was thrown up around Wyke and the king made stipulations about the thatched houses being tiled and vacant land being brought into use.

On 1st April 1299, Wyke was granted a Royal Charter and became known as the free borough of Kingston-upon-Hull. The charter granted the town certain privileges such as freedom from tolls in England for the burgesses and the confirming of the markets and fair. The king established his own court and a mint and the town was freed from the rule of the County sheriff, well-known for his use of torture and demands for money. Hull was governed at first by a Custodian until a new Charter of 1331 allowed the appointment of a Mayor. The first mayor was the wealthy Hull merchant William de la Pole. By 1302 the king had built a new quay, new merchants were being attracted to the town and in 1304 Hull sent its first two members to Parliament, Robert de Barton and Richard de Gretford. The foundations had been laid for the growth of a great port and city.

The years that followed the granting of the Charter in 1299 were ones of steady growth and improvement. Edward II allowed a portion of the town's tolls to be used to pave the streets and by 1315 there was a regular ferry crossing the Humber from Hull to Barton. An earlier ferry from Hessle to Barton charged ½d for foot passengers and 1d for a horseman.

The fourteenth and fifteenth century saw the growth of churches and religious houses in the town. Wealthy men felt it natural to give money to found monasteries and hospitals and to help erect or improve churches. This was not only seen as public spirited and bringing employment to the town but helped ensure a favourable reception in the after life.

We know that there was a simple chapel in 1230 on the site of the present Holy Trinity church and perhaps one where St Mary's Lowgate now stands. With the growth in population and status of the town, the simple chapels were no longer seen as suitable and with a gift of 20 shillings from John Skayl, (Scale Lane gets its name from him) in 1303, the rebuilding of Holy Trinity Church began, work which would not be completed until the early fifteenth century. The church is remarkable not only for its size, being one of the largest parish churches in the country, but for its use of brick in the construction and the church is now the oldest brick building in Britain still used for its original purpose. The first vicar was Robert de Martin who took up his position in 1324.

Right
Holy Trinity Church

The earliest mention of St Mary's church is in a will of 1327 when it was left 20 shillings by Nicholas Putfra, a merchant. Little more is known of the construction of the medieval church but in 1518 the west end of the church collapsed and the present church is the work of seventeenth and nineteenth century restorers.

As well as the two parish churches, Hull attracted monks and friars who began to settle in the town and build their monasteries and houses. In 1290 the Carmelites founded a friary with help from King Edward I, Sir Thomas Ughtred and Sir Richard de la Pole. The friary extended along the south side of Whitefriargate. The Black friars, or Austin Friars, came from York early in the fourteenth century to found their house on Marketgate. Their building lasted until the end of the eighteenth century when it was demolished. The Carthusians settled just to the north of Hull in 1354 with help from the de la Pole family. The last remnant of the Priory, the eastern gateway, was demolished in 1805.

The walls that were to enclose Hull were begun following an initiative from the citizens of the town who petitioned Edward II for permission to build, which was granted in 1321. No reason is given for the wish to have the walls built but with Scots marauders reaching York in 1319 and the town vulnerable from attack along its waterfront, the old ditch and moat were seen as inadequate defences in troubled times. The first section to be begun was along the Humber front. Nearly five million bricks were to be used in the construction and the design seems to draw inspiration from Eastern fortifications, which the engineers may have been familiar with. Gradually, the gateways and towers and a chain across the River Hull were added until the whole enterprise was completed at the end of the fourteenth century. Later plans of the town drawn in the seventeenth century clearly show the walls on three sides with further defences, including the first 'strong castle', across the River Hull to protect the east side. The walls last saw active service in 1745 when the Jacobite supporters of Charles Stuart were marching through the north of England and the Corporation mounted twenty cannon on the walls in case they came to Hull, which they did not. In later, more peaceful times, the walls fell into disrepair with only the south wall still standing by the early nineteenth century. Building work in the town constantly threw up the foundations and even the massive iron socket of the old north gate was discovered in 1853 when a south wing was added to the Dock Office.

The foundations of the North Gate were recently excavated and left on permanent display as a reminder of the once great walls of the city.

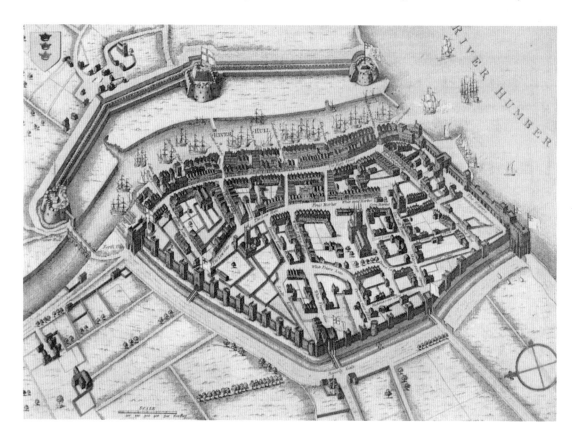

Above
Hull in the 17th Century showing the Medieval Walls

The fourteenth and fifteenth centuries were a boom time for Hull as the main port for Yorkshire's expanding wool and cloth trade. Cloth took over from wool as the main export during the fifteenth century. By 1393, 3,000 rolls of cloth a year were leaving Hull to markets as diverse as Spain, the Netherlands and Venice. The fish trade with Iceland grew in importance during the fifteenth century. Ships were still relatively small, the majority of them being between 20 and 30 tons with the occasional exceptionally large ship, such as the *Anthony*, weighing 400 tons. The ships increasingly moved in convoys for fear of pirates and capture by enemy ships in time of war. Hull, indeed, had its own pirates, preying on enemy ships. John Tutbury captured a Prussian ship in 1402 and Hugh Clitheroe, who had been Mayor four times, was repeatedly arrested for boarding foreign ships.

Left
A Medieval
ship enters the
Humber

Above
Weavers making
cloth to be exported
from Hull

It was during the fourteenth century that the Bubonic Plague or 'black death' came to England, first appearing in Dorset in 1348. It reached Hull in 1349 when an estimated half of the population died but the tax returns for 1377 show a population of nearly 1,600 clustered around Hull Street and Marketgate. The numbers were probably made up by workers coming in from the countryside attracted by the high wages and cheap accommodation caused by the lack of workers who had died.

Not that life in the town would have been pleasant for them, by modern standards. With no sanitation and open sewers and animals kept within the walls, the smell must have been overpowering. However, Hull was no worse than most towns of the period and in some ways better. At least there was a river where sewage and rubbish could be tipped and swept away by the tides and Hollar's engraving of Hull from 1640 still shows open ground and gardens away from the built up areas around the river.

As in most towns in Medieval England the merchants, traders and craftsmen formed themselves into Guilds. The Guilds had many purposes. In a time of sudden death and fluctuating trade, each member would pay into a common fund which could be drawn on by widows or when a ship had been lost or captured. The craftsmen took on apprentices who would be trained and standards of workmanship were maintained by the masters. The bigger Guilds would use their influence to petition the Monarchy and Corporation for privileges, designed to keep 'strangers' from trading in the town or to restrict the import of goods from other towns or from abroad, if it was thought this would drive down prices. The most powerful early Guild in Hull was the Holy Trinity Guild, based at the church and run by the ship owners. It numbered 250 members in 1398 and ran an alms house for poor mariners. It gradually increased its influence over everything to do with shipping and the port and by 1512 it ran the pilot service up and down the Humber. The Hull Merchants' Company, a later guild existed from 1499 to 1706 and virtually monopolised all trade in the town.

Right
King Richard II

In 1399 national events involved Hull. Henry Bolingbroke landed at Ravenser (now washed away by the North Sea) on the East coast and marched inland in his attempt to take over the crown from Richard II. The mayor of Hull, John Tutbury, declared for Richard, who had granted Hull many new privileges and would not allow Henry entry into the town. Unfortunately for Hull, Richard was defeated by Henry and assassinated. The new King Henry IV, was placated by the townsmen led by Michael de la Pole and no long-term damage seems to have been done to the town's relationships with the crown.

1440 was an important year for Hull. King Henry VI, made Hull an independent county, allowed to elect its own Sheriff and 13 Aldermen as a Corporation to run the town, one of whom was to be elected Mayor. This new Corporation not only governed Hull but absorbed the outlying villages of Hessle, North Ferriby, Kirk Ella, Swanland, Willerby and Anlaby. This remained the position until 1835. Despite its elevated position, the new Corporation had difficulty maintaining its independence from the feudal lords competing for the crown of England in the Wars of the Roses. Many could be bribed and flattered but in 1460 Egremont, a younger son of the Percy family, attacked the town with a small army trying to enforce his supposed rights to collect taxes. The citizens had to man the walls and parley with him until a decision could be had from London which found in the Corporation's favour and Egremont withdrew ungraciously, uttering threats. Similarly, Lord Montague threatened John Green, the mayor, that he would be 'chopped as small as flesh to pot' for imprisoning some of his men who had rampaged through Hull. The mayor was murdered later that year.

At the close of the Middle Ages in 1485, Hull would have been a town with a variety of buildings. Dominating the town was Holy Trinity Church and the house of the de la Pole family, the manor house, which with its tower and many chambers and valuable fittings was the most impressive house in the town. It stood in present day Manor Street. The Corporation met in the Guildhall in the Market Place and there was a school near to Holy Trinity Church as early as 1347. The predecessor of the Grammar School was established by the Corporation in 1479 who paid for the master. The schoolroom was built on land donated by the Alcock family to the south of Holy Trinity Church. Houses were a mixture of wooden framed buildings filled with wattle and daub and with a central hearth, letting smoke out of the roof and brick built dwellings with chimneys. Brick making, carried on outside the walls, was a major industry in Hull and some cloth was woven but Hull was primarily a port rather than a manufacturing town. The jetty had been extensively repaired and stone was taking the place of the old wooden piles. A fresh water ditch had been dug from a source in Anlaby to supply the town with water and thought was being given to the town's sanitary arrangements. It was forbidden to use the river Hull as a latrine. Latrine holes were stopped up and a public toilet was built at some expense and a salaried official appointed to keep a two-wheeled muck cart to remove refuse from the town. The massive walls were the most striking feature of the town and although the citizens were not adverse to helping themselves to bricks from it, they were to serve the town well in the coming centuries.

Right
The Port of Hull at the end of the Middle Ages

Michael de la Pole

The de la Pole family traded in Hull from the beginning of the fourteenth century and were probably of Welsh origin. Michael was born in 1330 and during his twenties spent much time fighting for Edward III in France, where he was twice taken prisoner. When Edward died in 1377, Michael became a favourite of the new young King, Richard II and at the age of 52 became the Chancellor of all England. In 1385 he was made Earl of Suffolk but when he fell out of favour with Richard he was forced to flee to Paris via Hull where he died in poverty in 1389.

TUDOR HULL

When Henry Tudor was victorious over Richard III at the battle of Bosworth in 1485 and began the Tudor family's long occupation of the English throne, reaction in Hull was mixed. There may well have been some sympathy for Richard who was a local magnate but safe behind their walls, the townsmen got on with the day-to-day problems of life and the serious business of making money. There were felons to be apprehended and tried and the owner of a ship which had sunk in the mouth of the Hull to be traced.

National concerns were not to impinge on Hull until the reign of Henry VIII, which began in 1509. In need of money to fight his wars and a divorce from his first wife to secure a male heir to the throne, Henry turned his attention to the wealth of the church. He began by confiscating smaller religious houses and then the larger.

Left Henry VIII

Closures of monasteries and nunneries took place all over the country as Henry's need for money, mixed with the new ideas of the Reformation, to bring about mass confiscations of church property and brutality against any who dared to voice opposition to the reforms. No one was safe, from Thomas More the chancellor who was executed in 1535 to humble friars who were burned for refusing to accept the king's authority.

The backlash against these changes came in the north of England and was known as the 'Pilgrimage of Grace'. Under their leader, Robert Aske, a huge army of 40,000 men backed by leading northern aristocrats, like the Percys, demanded the restoration of the monasteries and the end of reform. Hull declared for the king and would not allow the rebels to enter the town, so in the October of 1536, they surrounded Hull and demanded entry. Negotiations followed and eventually the rebels were allowed to enter the town peacefully. Faced with so large a rebellion, Henry backed down, promising the Pilgrims all they asked at a meeting in Doncaster but once they had dispersed he moved quickly to round up and execute the leaders and a proportion of the population of every town and village involved. Hull was now in a difficult position as it had technically joined the rebellion although not actively taken part. One rebel, John Hallam, was hung from the town walls in chains and left to die but otherwise Hull was part of the general pardon that followed the end of the 'Pilgrimage of Grace'.

In Hull, the White and Black friars' houses were dissolved in 1539 and then in 1547 the chantries based at Holy Trinity Church and St Mary's were closed and their revenues confiscated. Holy Trinity Church was stripped of all its statues and paintings which were publicly burned. However, the hospital based at the Carthusian Monastery was saved and transferred to the ownership of the Corporation. Similarly, the Corporation successfully petitioned for the return of the revenues used to support the Grammar School and in 1563 the area of the school was enlarged. With the support of the merchant William Cree, a new building was constructed for the school in 1585 and it is this building which still stands in the market place, although the school has long since moved to modern buildings.

Henry came in person to Hull twice in 1541 to see to the town's fortifications which were considered inadequate against possible foreign attack and occupation. He ordered repairs and improvements to the walls, a castle to be built on the east bank of the river Hull and also the first bridge across the river. Stone was fetched from the ruins of Meaux Abbey which had been closed and left to fall into ruin. The work was complete by the end of 1543 at a cost of £23,000. The fortifications were handed over to the town in 1552 with a grant of £50 a year for their upkeep. The castle was massive with walls fifteen feet thick, designed to resist any bombardment from the Humber.

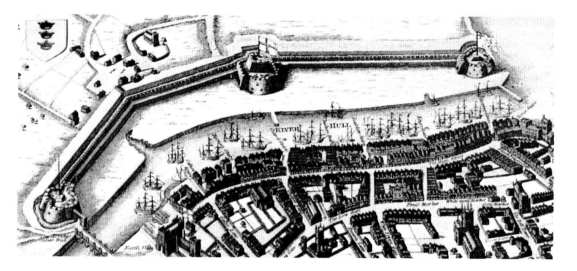

Henry's daughter, Queen Elizabeth I, never visited Yorkshire but she was expected in Hull in 1575 and the town set about tidying itself up, painting houses and carting away rubbish. The change from Medieval to 'modern' was gradual. Brick became the predominant building material and thatch gave way to tile, a factor which was to prevent any serious fires in the town. Ordnances were frequently issued by the Corporation to improve life in the town. The number of farm animals allowed to be kept within the walls was restricted, as was the building of privies discharging into the river. When plague struck again in 1575, the infected streets were barricaded off and movements and gatherings banned until it had died away. There were outbreaks of the plague again in 1602-4 and 1637. In the last outbreak perhaps 10% of the population died including the mayor. The dike bringing fresh water to the town was regularly cleaned and provision was made for it to be inspected weekly.

The great crisis of Elizabeth's reign was the imminent threat of invasion from The Netherlands which were then owned by Spain. Because of its position opposite Holland, the Humber was seen as a likely landing place for the barges containing the invasion army and money was spent by the central government and by the town council ensuring the new defences were kept in good repair and well provisioned with armaments. As a sea port, Hull was expected to provide armed ships for the defence of the realm, although the cost was shared out between other Yorkshire towns such as York. When the Armada sailed from Spain in 1588, as the first part of the invasion plan, three ships from Hull manned by two hundred sailors were provided and they joined the English fleet which opposed the Armada. Again in 1595, Hull fitted out the *Elizabeth Jonas* which took part in the successful raid on Cadiz. Hull ships were often used to transport troops to the Continent in support of England's allies there.

The town Corporation was increasingly becoming puritan-minded and would issue ordnances ordering people to be good, 'they do thunder out the manifold, grievous and terrible plagues of God hanging over this town if a speedy reformation be not had', but could do nothing to stop the growth of public houses of which there were thirty-nine in 1574 supplied by ten brewers. By 1599 all plays whether by amateurs or professionals were banned from the town. The poor continued to trouble the members of the Corporation, especially when the price of corn was high and they could not afford bread. There were forty places in the town's alms houses for the poor but to prevent begging, food was handed out and attempts made to put the unemployed to work in various trades such as knitting.

Although there was some small scale manufacturing in the town, this was largely for local consumption to supply the population which had reached 5,000 by 1576. The exception was ship building which can be traced to 1567 in the town when John Hodgkinson leased land for a slipway. He was joined by others as the century progressed. Trade continued to be Hull's life blood with fish from Iceland and later whale oil from the Baltic added to the list of commodities imported and exported through the town. Hull ships took part in whaling off Norway once they had acquired the skills needed to chase the whales but this new initiative ended in 1623 when the Privy Council in London forbad further whaling from Hull in that region in favour of the London Muscovy Company who claimed the monopoly of the trade but Hull whalers were still active in the seas around Greenland.

Thomas Whincup

We know from his memorial statue in Holy Trinity Church that Thomas Whincup was born in 1550 and died in 1624. His appointment was 'lecturer', that is he would speak to the congregation, often at great length, on some learned topic of protestant theology and to make sure everyone attended and none escaped, the town's gates were locked during the service. In 1599 the Archbishop of York delegated his power to try moral offenders to Whincup and cases of drunkenness and lewdness were brought before him. Whincup's stern Protestantism was typical of the rulers of Hull in Tudor times.

STUART HULL

Elizabeth died in 1603 to be succeeded by her nephew James Stuart, who was also king of Scotland. James travelled slowly down through England on his way to London and the Mayor, Mr Barnard, with the town clerk and Hull's leading merchant, William Gee, travelled from Hull to York to pledge their allegiance to the new king on behalf of the town.

All was not well in Hull in the early part of the seventeenth century. Apart from the regular return of the plague which isolated the town, forcing merchants to look for alternative ports to ship their produce, the overall level of trade was falling. There was competition from foreign manufacturers of cloth and heavy duties were imposed by foreign monarchs, designed to raise revenue and protect their own industries. The new Gainsborough fair was attracting buyers from London and was supplying the markets of Yorkshire and Derbyshire previously supplied by Hull. The fishing and whaling trade was in decline and when James and his son Charles I made demands for money and forced loans from Hull, the town pleaded poverty.

Hollar's view of Hull in 1640 (page 8) still shows the town within its walls and moat, dominated by Holy Trinity Church in the centre of the town. The manor house with its massive tower and St Mary's Church, which was now towerless since the fall of the tower in 1518, were the other main buildings. Most of the housing was clustered along the river with many open spaces away from the riverside. The streets were largely cobbled and piped water had come to those houses which could afford it in 1612, when a horse powered pump was set up by John Revell and John Cater.

The town and council were almost entirely Puritan and resisted pressures to conform to the anti-puritan views of William Laud, the Archbishop of Canterbury. The few Catholics were looked at suspiciously and even imprisoned over the river in the citadel for refusing to attend Church of England services.

Relations between King Charles and his Parliament in London deteriorated to such an extent that Charles fled the capital in March 1642 and moved his family and court to York making it, in effect, the capital of England. Charles had tried to rule without Parliament from 1629 to 1640 and had levied an increasing number of what were seen as excessive and unjust taxes, which caused resentment throughout the country. The king left York on the 16 August for Nottingham leaving a garrison of 4,000 soldiers under the Duke of Newcastle. At Nottingham the king raised his standard, declaring the opening of hostilities between himself and Parliament and the beginning of the civil war, which would only end with the king's execution in 1649.

Left
Charles I

At the start of the war, the north of England was almost entirely in support of the king but the position of Hull was crucial. Not only did it have arms, including 200,000 muskets and fifty cannon and powder in store but more importantly was crucially placed to receive help from the king's relatives and supporters in Europe. The king had inspected Hull's defences and preparations in a two day visit to the town in 1639, when he was preparing for his war with Scotland. He lodged in Sir John Lister's house in the High Street, the house later to be rebuilt as the Wilberforce House.

However, it was by no means clear who Hull would support in the coming war. The King's Governor in the town, Sir Thomas Glemham had been replaced by Sir John Hotham who had been appointed by Parliament but his loyalty was uncertain. The Mayor, Henry Barnard, was for the king as were 'five parts off seven' according to Hotham.

Matters were brought to a head on Saturday 23rd April 1642 when Hotham received a letter informing him that King Charles intended to dine with him that day. Hotham conferred with Peregrine Pelham, the M.P. for Hull, a known Parliament man and some of the town's aldermen but not the Mayor. They met at the White Harte Inn off Silver Street in a room, which came to be known as the 'plotting parlour'. Hotham had clear instructions from Parliament not to surrender the town and secure behind the walls and with a garrison of over 1,000 men he took the dramatic step of refusing the King entry into the town when Charles and his retinue arrived at Beverley Gate. The outraged king retired to York to prepare his forces. Although not a shot had been fired, the civil war may be said to have begun in earnest with John Hotham's refusal to obey the king's order.

Right
Sir John Hotham refuses Charles I entry into Hull

There were two sieges of Hull in July 1642 and in the following year from 2 September to 11th October. Both were doomed to failure. With control of the navy, Parliament could easily reinforce Hull with men and supplies and water was still drinkable from the River Hull. Moreover, the protective dykes were cut, flooding the countryside around Hull, making it impossible to dig siege positions and making life very unpleasant for the besieging forces. The garrison was able to make lightning raids from Hull, inflict heavy losses on the King's troops and then retire behind the walls.

Despite these successes for Hotham, he and his son Captain John Hotham, began to make arrangements to change sides and join the king. Perhaps the Hothams' pride had been hurt when Lord Fairfax was made Parliament's commander-in-chief in the north or perhaps they judged the war would eventually be won by the king. Their plotting was uncovered and Captain Hotham was arrested in Hull and John Hotham in Beverley, trying to escape to his fortified house in Scorborough. Both men were taken by ship from Hull to London and executed. Parliament appointed Lord Fairfax as governor of the town and he led his troops in a final battle against the besiegers on the 11th of October. He was completely victorious and Hull was not troubled again.

Left
Lord Thomas Fairfax

Casualties and damage to the town had been relatively light and the population had increased to 6,500 by 1652. However, much trade had been lost during the sieges and the town was increasingly called upon to supply money, men and ships to fight in the war. Many individuals who had supported the king were heavily fined by Parliament. Henry Hildyard, for example, was fined £14,742 equivalent to two years' of his income.

Although Hull was largely a puritan town, it divided itself into two religious camps. One followed the more extreme type of Puritanism and was supported by the town garrison, while the other more moderate party was made up of the townspeople. Both camps had its own preachers and matters came to the point where a wall was built in Holy Trinity Church so that both sides could worship in their own manner without interference from the other.

The reign of Parliament and Oliver Cromwell was short, from 1649 to 1660 and despite its Puritan and Parliamentary sympathies, Hull accepted the return of Charles' son as Charles II with prudent good grace. The Corporation held a banquet for the new governor, Lord Bellasis, although he was Catholic and £45 was allowed out of the Corporation's iron chest for a public feast to celebrate the coronation of Charles II.

A new Charter was negotiated in 1661 which removed many of the town's rulers who were felt to be unsympathetic to the new order but most of the old privileges were secured and the charter lasted until 1835. Parliamentary elections in 1661 returned the Royalist, Anthony Gylby, as one of Hull's members but surprisingly, the poet Andrew Marvell was also returned. Marvell had served in the Parliaments of 1649 to 1660 and was disliked by the court in London but he had the backing of the Corporation and he continued to serve until his death in 1678.

Feelings against Charles II quickly deteriorated in Hull. Charles had allied himself with Louis XIV of France in a war against Holland and trading towns along the east coast soon felt the effects of Dutch sea power at a time when the Royal Navy had been allowed to run down. Dutch warships roaming the North Sea were preventing trading ships from leaving port unless in a protected convoy and a Dutch privateer came into the Humber in 1672. Britain made peace with Holland in 1674 and the town's true sympathies were clear when two ships sailed from Hull with over a hundred men to fight with the Dutch against France, despite a royal proclamation banning enlistment.

Charles died in 1685 to be succeeded by his brother James II. James was a devout catholic and there had been attempts to stop him succeeding to the throne, attempts supported by the majority on Hull's Corporation. Acts of Parliament banning nonconformists from meeting had limited success in Hull where the mayor and members of the Corporation stayed behind after the formal service in Holy Trinity Church to hear George Acklam, a nonconformist preacher, give a sermon. Other similar preachers drew large crowds and as early as 1659 the town's Quakers were being prosecuted for refusing to pay taxes, which supported the parish churches or 'steeple houses' as Quakers called them. Perhaps two-thirds of the town were Presbyterians, radicals who saw the congregation as the source of power, rather than bishops and the ministers. James removed all but one of the aldermen in 1688 and replaced them with his own followers but was forced to allow them back when support began to grow for the protestant William of Orange.

When it became clear that William had enough support to be able to take over the crown from James, he began to assemble an army in Holland. The north of England was a likely landing place and Hull and its garrison were crucial. The Catholic governor of the citadel, Marmaduke Langdale, hung the chain across the river and flooded the countryside. The garrison's Protestant officers secretly met the town Corporation who agreed to arm the population and that night Langdale and all the Catholic officers were arrested and placed in the fort, along with the town's Catholics. There was little violence and the looting of Catholic houses was quickly suppressed. 'Town taking day' was celebrated in Hull well into the eighteenth century. With the coronation of a Protestant king, nonconformists could worship openly and a Presbyterian Chapel was built in Bowlalley Lane in 1698. Catholics all but disappeared from Hull.

Hull was beginning to prosper again with the end of the Dutch wars and the growth of the Baltic trade largely channelled through the port. Hull was now the third port in the kingdom after London and Bristol and the population reached 7,000 by the end of the 17th century. The merchants began to build fine houses of brick of which the present Wilberforce House is a surviving example. During the late 17th century, the castle and South Blockhouse were incorporated within the design of Hull Citadel - a rare pure bastioned artillery fort roughly triangular in plan.

Below
Wilberforce House

By 1682 there were some forty shipbuilders and repairers in the town, the most prominent being the Blayde family who grew rich by building and repairing ships for the navy.

Conditions for the poor hardly changed and may even have deteriorated. Conditions of work were tilted in favour of the masters, strikes being banned and in 1697 a 'House of Correction' was built where the poor could be housed and set to work. The plague did not return but poor sanitation and grinding poverty kept the death rate high, forty-one percent more people dying in Hull than being born in 1689.

Andrew Marvell

Andrew Marvell was born in 1621 at Winestead and educated at Hull Grammar School. He was Milton's assistant and began writing his own poetry. In 1659 he was elected Member of Parliament for Hull, for which the town paid him a salary. He took a firmly republican stand even at the restoration of Charles II when such thoughts were unpopular. He remained the MP for Hull until his death in London in 1678.

'Had we but world enough, and time,
This coyness, Lady, were no crime.
We would sit down and think which way
To walk and pass our long love's day.
Thou by the Indian Ganges' side
Shouldst rubies find: I by the tide
Of Humber would complain.'

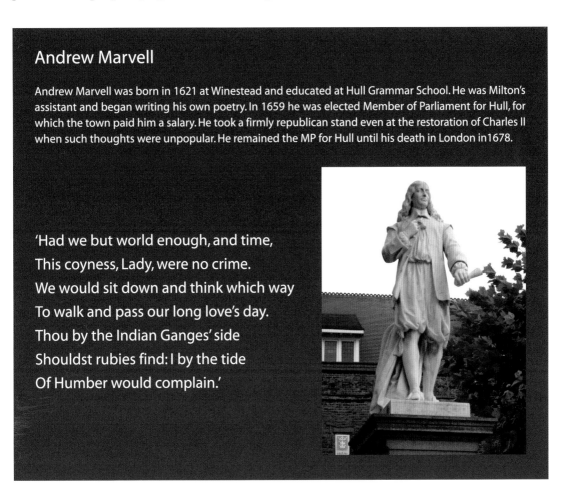

HULL IN THE EIGHTEENTH CENTURY

The eighteenth century was one of rapid growth for Hull. In 1700 the population stood at some 7,000 and this grew to around 22,000 by 1800. As ever, it was the impetus of expanding trade that gave Hull this accelerated growth. Increasing populations throughout Britain and Europe increased the demands for the import of raw materials such as iron from Sweden and Russia and the export of finished goods such as cutlery from Sheffield and cloth from the expanding towns of West Yorkshire. In 1788, 1,058 ships used the port and this increased by fifty per cent in just four years. From 1783 to 1793, customs revenues increased from £86,000 to £200,000. With the beginnings of the Industrial Revolution and the increased output from the factories of Lancashire and Yorkshire, Hull was well placed to profit from this expanding trade.

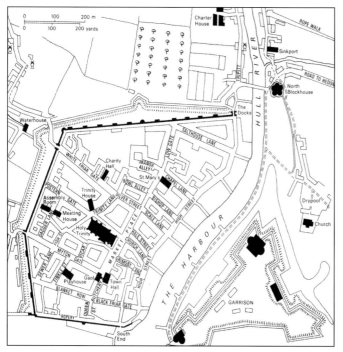

Above
Hull in the 18th
Century

The growth in population meant inevitable change as the pressure on the space within the walls for housing and warehousing began to fill in the available sites. Hull was still contained within its walls on the west side of the river Hull with the citadel and its garrison occupying the east bank. The bridge across the Hull described by Daniel Defoe in 1726 as, 'a noble stone bridge ...consisting of fourteen arches', was to the north of the town, outside the wall and guarded by the citadel's north blockhouse. Incidentally, Defoe had his famous hero, Robinson Crusoe, setting off on his first eventful voyage from Hull.

The initial expansion of the town took place within the walls. The old butter cross in the market place was demolished in 1761 followed by the market house and the gaol. Priest Row was demolished and a new street, King Street, laid out. Mytongate spread beyond the walls into Castle Street. Whitefriargate was linked to the new Quay Street at the end of the century by Parliament Street. This was built by private enterprise and the houses erected there were meant for the well-off with rents of up to £25 a year.

A statue was raised to King William III in 1734 showing him in Roman costume on a fine horse, all gilded. The statue was originally commissioned from the artist, Pieter Scheemaker of London, by the town of Bristol but was eventually bought by Hull Corporation and generous individuals for £837. 14s. 10d. It was placed at the south end of the market where it remained until the start of the second world war when it was removed to Houghton Hall, near Sancton to protect it from the feared bombing. It was returned to its plinth in 1949. Many Hull stories are still told about 'King Billy' including one that says the sculptor committed suicide because he forgot to include the spurs. This is far from the truth as Scheemaker died in 1770 from unknown causes and as the statue was a copy of a classical Roman work, it would not have had spurs, which the Romans did not use. Another legend has William leaving his horse and wondering down to the river, a story which probably has more to do with Hull's famous strong beer than any supernatural causes.

Already by the beginning of the century, the increasing traffic was churning up the streets of the town to such an extent that the Corporation had to bring in regulations to fix the width of wheeled vehicles to nine inches. Many small goods were still transported around on sleds, which could negotiate the cobbled streets easier than wheeled vehicles. It was not until 1825 that the new macadamised system for paving roads was introduced to Hull, Wellington Street being the first to be converted.

.

From 1755 the town Corporation passed a number of 'Improvement Acts' designed to tackle the worst of the town's problems. Shopkeepers were forbidden to use the pavements to display their goods and householders who built steps and bow windows out onto the streets were restricted to twenty-two inches. Gradually, the medieval central gutter was replaced by gutters to either side of the street and during the 1760s the main streets of the town began to have flagged pavements for pedestrians. Name plates were fixed onto houses at the corner of streets. The Corporation took over responsibility for piping water into the town by buying up the privately owned pumping station. At first the main pipes were made of wood with lead pipes leading off into the houses but cast iron began to replace wood by 1819 and the horse powered pump was replaced by one of the new steam powered pumps. Similarly, street lighting was introduced in 1762, fuelled by whale oil. Before that, the only lights at night where the ones provided by candles at the front doors of houses. The Corporation had little power to raise money for all these reforms, relying on its income from tolls and dues and not until 1762 was it possible to overcome opposition and raise a limited rate or tax on property. The usual procedure was to rely on a joint effort with house owners who wished to have their streets improved, the Corporation providing the material and the householders paying for the workmen.

Right
A Cobbled Lane
with side gutters

It soon became clear that the haven of the River Hull was too small to cope with the increasing river traffic and the increasing size of the ships coming into port. Despite some opposition from those who profited from the lax customs collections along the old haven banks and who were heavily involved in smuggling, a Dock Act of 1774 allowed the building of a new dock to the north of the town, financed by the selling of shares and by 1778 the Hull whaler *Manchester* was the first to enter the new dock. The dock covered ten acres and was for a time, the biggest dock in England but was not officially named the Queen's Dock until 1854 when Queen Victoria and Prince Albert visited Hull. This first dock saw service until 1935 when it was filled in and transformed into the Queen's Gardens.

The building of the new dock meant the demolition of the northern walls and earth removed for the building of the dock was spread out and formed the foundation of a new suburb with the building of George Street, Charlotte Street and Bond Street.

Left
Wilberforce looks down on to the Queen's Gardens

By the end of the eighteenth century Hull had been linked to Liverpool, Birmingham, Bristol and London by canal, a large factor in the enormous increase in trade which was to pick up again in the nineteenth century once the Napoleonic wars were over and trade was flowing. At the beginning of the eighteenth century Hull was still relatively isolated. The roads connecting the town to the rest of the country were poor. Even the farmers from Cottingham to the west of Hull, had to bring their produce into town on horseback rather than cart because of the state of the roads and there was no direct road to Hedon to the east of the town. Private companies set up turnpike roads and charged fees and this meant some improvement of the local roads. The Hull to Beverley turnpike road was opened in 1744 and was still charging tolls on the road in 1871. There was a stage coach connection to York and by the end of the century the journey time from York to London had been cut from four days to thirty-six hours. Real improvements to the roads would not be made until the next century.

Below
The Hull to Beverley
Stage Coach

Eighteenth century politics were boisterous and impossibly corrupt by modern standards and Hull was no exception. Votes at Parliamentary elections were openly on sale for two guineas and when in 1812 only two candidates stood for Hull's two seats, the poorer freemen, who had the right to vote, accosted a perfect stranger in the streets of Beverley and persuaded him to stand, forcing the original two candidates to bribe the electors in the usual way. Hull's MPs were a mixed lot. Lord Robert Manners served for thirty-five years but never made a speech in the House of Commons while the best known MP, William Wilberforce, who was born in Hull in 1759, was one of the driving forces behind the movement for the abolition of slavery and was the main spokesman and organiser in Parliament.

For the greater part of the population of Hull, life was hard and relatively short and such 'entertainment' as there was, was to be found in the churches and chapels or inns, where cock fighting took place and on public occasions such as the opening of the docks or an election to Parliament. The annual fair and visiting circuses from 1785 provided welcome entertainment for a mass audience. But for those with the money and the leisure to spare and who had travelled to York or London and had seen the theatres, gardens and assembly rooms on offer there, Hull must have seemed 'rather provincial'. There may have been a theatre in Whitefriargate as early as early as 1600 but no records have been found but by 1743 the 'New Theatre' had been established in Lowgate, owned by Thomas Keregan. In 1769 Tate Wilkinson built a theatre in Finkle Street, to become the town's 'Theatre Royal', attracting some of the country's leading actors including Mrs Sissons. The fashionable portrait painters John Russell and William Chamberlain found employment in the town and there were musical evenings at the Neptune Inn. Newspapers could be read at Sam's Coffee House on Church Side and for those not influenced by the town's 'committee for the suppression of vice' there was an army of prostitutes who frequented the inns, theatre and the horse races held in Newington.

The war with France, which ran from 1793 until 1815, brought hard times for the poor of Hull. Hull was supposed to find 731 men as its quota for the Navy but there were few volunteers and the press gang was at work in the streets of Hull. In 1794 the Hull whaler *Sarah and Elizabeth* was stopped at sea by the frigate *Aurora* and most of the crew were pressed into the navy but only after two of them had been killed in the struggle. The *Aurora's* Captain, Essington, was later cleared when all the papers relating to the case were lost. If the navy could be avoided, the call up to the militia was more difficult and only those able to find the £40 needed to pay for a substitute, could escape.

With the continental ports blockaded, the price of bread rose and there was unemployment. As early as 1789, one eighth of the population was dependent on the Corporation's payment of one shilling per family a week. There were riots in 1796 and again in 1802, when the price of flour rose, and the Riot Act was read. The militia based at the fort were often called out to maintain order in the streets. Two shoemakers, Thompson and Smith were sent to prison for nine months for trying to form a union to raise wages and cases of dysentery, caused by poor diet, were reported in almost three-quarters of the population of Hull. As late as May 1815 there was a riot when the mob rescued a man from the press gang and wrecked the local pub for good measure.

The gap between rich and poor was becoming more marked. At one point the poor were not even being given a burial below ground but were being stacked up against a wall at Holy Trinity Church while at the same time the Eggington brothers, oil-mill owners, were buying a 500 acre estate for £14,750.

Like many other growing towns of the eighteenth century, Hull was struggling to cope with the problems of rapid expansion. The Corporation's record of reform is commendable but the days of an unelected, body of wealthy men, serving for life and running the town as they saw fit, could not long stand the calls for reform which were to come in the next century.

William Wilberforce

William Wilberforce was born in Hull in 1759 into one of the town's wealthy merchant families. He was elected MP for Hull in 1784 and until his retirement from Parliament in 1825 he led the fight against the slave trade. A life long evangelical Christian, he worked alongside Quakers and others and in 1807 succeeded in having slavery abolished in the British Empire. He then continued to work for the total abolition of slavery. He died in 1833 and was buried in Westminster Abbey. Wilberforce House in Hull is a museum to his life and work.

William Wilberforce

HULL IN THE NINETEENTH CENTURY

The system of governing the town had hardly changed since the Middle Ages with all effective powers being in the hands of the thirteen aldermen, elected for life, who in turn chose the Mayor. The right to vote for Parliamentary elections was in the hands of the 'burgesses', a right passed on from father to son or earned through serving a lengthy apprenticeship of even bought outright for sums as high as 250 guineas.

In 1832 the system for electing the House of Commons was changed to bring in middle class men and to allocate the seats in the House more in line with the actual population of Britain. Local government could not be far behind. Calls for reform of the Corporation began in the 1830s led by a flamboyant radical, James Acland, who attacked the Corporation in his newspaper the *Hull Portfolio*. He was adept at public relations, refusing to pay the Corporation's tolls and selling 'anti-corporate tea' and 'public opinion coffee'. Along with others, Hull Corporation was investigated by a Parliamentary Commission which criticised the secrecy and financial affairs of the Corporation. In 1835 the old Corporation was abolished and a new one, almost entirely Liberal in its make-up of twenty-eight councillors, was elected by the ratepayers of the town. The new Corporation took over responsibility for fire-prevention, lighting, paving and drainage.

One of Hull's most urgent problems was the treatment of the growing number of the poor. The national government allowed the setting up of workhouses where the poor could be housed and fed but in conditions which would be worse than the poorest who were employed outside the hated buildings. Hull had two workhouses, one for Hull parish on the corner of Parliament Street and Whitefriargate and one for Sculcoates on Beverley Road. Paupers were set to work doing menial tasks or breaking stones. Conditions in the Hull workhouse were so poor that a quarter of the inmates died in 1847 and a new workhouse was built on Anlaby Road in 1852. This system endured until 1929 when the Beverley Road workhouse became the Kingston General Hospital and the Anlaby Road workhouse the Hull Royal Infirmary.

Right Hull Workhouse

Living conditions for the poor in Hull were as bad as any other industrial town of the century and outbreaks of cholera and typhus were frequent visitors; nearly half of all deaths in 1841 were children under five years of age. The Medical Society of Hull reported in 1847 and described 'overcrowded living conditions, stinking dunghills, muck garths and pigs and their evil-smelling sties and the overbursting graveyard of St Mary's, Lowgate.' In 1849 cholera killed 1,860 inhabitants, 500 in one week alone. The responsible authorities were slow to act and there is strong evidence that corrupt councillors and officials acted in their own interests rather than those they were elected to represent. It was not certain at the time what the causes of the diseases were, let alone what the cure was. Polluted water was the cause of cholera and not until Hull's drinking water was supplied from the pure source at Springhead, identified by William Warden, a plumber from Hessle, and the burial of the dead moved to the new cemetery on Spring Bank, did the position improve. Hull's inadequate sanitary system still relied on earth toilets and the removal of 'night soil' in carts to 'muck garths' which infested the town. The many horses and stables in the town attracted swarms of flies. A cow shed still stood at the corner of Craven Street in 1920. Drink and drugs were heavily taken by the poorer members of society who could least afford it, despite the efforts of the Temperance Movement to provide alternatives to the inns. Scarlet fever returned in 1881 carrying off 689 children.

By the middle of the century, Hull had been described as 'a gigantic slum'. Newcomers were attracted to the town by the relatively high wages on offer in the factories, cotton mills and dockyards and came from as far as Ireland as well as the surrounding countryside. They would work for lower wages than Hull workers and crowded into miserable courtyards and tenements in often squalid conditions. In Howard's Row in Sutton Bank, 300 people lived in twenty small houses. In a total population of some 95,000 there were 2268 seamen, 1000 engineers, 2100 labourers, 3200 domestic servants, 2188 cotton operatives and 627 prostitutes.

With such a high working class population, it is not surprising that Hull was a 'radical' town, giving support to the Chartist movement which demanded votes for working men and staging a series of successful strikes which demanded higher wages. When the new Labour Party came into existence Hull soon elected Labour councillors and an almost unbroken line of Labour M.Ps. to the present day

Schooling for children was patchy. There were a number of small private schools for the middle classes but provision for the poor was inadequate. Although Hull had 27 schools in 1859, this did not give every child a place and most attended only for about three years. The Catholic Convent on Anlaby Road was particularly successful - with forty nuns and 2,500 children attending. School attendance however, was not free and many children were put to work as soon as possible to help the family income. It would not be until Forster's Education Act of 1870 and the establishment of the Hull School Board that there was sufficient schooling. The Board built thirty-three schools including three schools at Brunswick Avenue, Boulevard and Craven Street which provided a secondary education for 3,000 pupils.

Left
Most children worked
as soon as possible

The end of the eighteenth century and the beginning of the nineteenth saw Hull burst its boundaries and begin to spread beyond its Medieval confines. Growth still continued within the old town. By 1804 the last remains of the town walls along the Humber were torn down and Wellington Street, Nelson Street and Pier Street were laid out on land reclaimed from the Humber. But the growth in population from 22,000 in 1801 to over 220,000 in 1900 meant that the town would be transformed beyond recognition. Radiating out from the old town, new roads and avenues would be built in a frenzy of building activity as speculators supplied the demand for housing for all sectors of the growing population. With few building regulations, the temptation was to pack as many dwellings as possible on the land available and this burst of building activity threw up many of the slum dwellings that were to be slowly cleared in the next century.

Below
Terraced Houses
on Hessle Road

The problem for shipping trying to enter the new dock was that it still had to negotiate the congestion of the old Haven. One skipper remarked that it took him longer to get from the Humber to the dock than to get from St Petersburg to the Humber. The solution was two new docks, linking the Queen's Dock directly with the Humber and avoiding the River Hull. These two docks, the Humber Dock, opened in 1809 and the Junction Dock in 1829, freed the congestion around the River Hull although the bridge linking the Queens' Dock with the Junction Dock caused traffic problems as it was opened to allow ships through. The Junction Dock was renamed the Prince's Dock after the royal visit in 1854 and saw service until 1968 when it was closed to shipping. It was later redeveloped and opened as Prince's Quay Shopping area in 1991. The Hull Dock Company saw the tonnage of ships entering its docks increase from 811,000 in 1850 to 2,258,000 in 1876 and the Hull based Wilson shipping company had forty-two steamers and was destined to become the world's largest shipping fleet. The new docks relieved the pressure on the River Hull traffic and this took on a new lease of life when seed crushing mills were built, able to take on their raw materials from barges. By 1878 there were forty-five mills crushing thousands of tons of linseed, cotton seed and rape seed.

Below
Hull's New Docks

As well as the regular imports of raw materials and the export of finished goods, Hull's involvement in the Greenland whaling trade increased dramatically in the nineteenth century. Throughout the previous century, Hull ships had gone whaling with some success but a government subsidy encouraged ship owners to fit out ships as whalers and by the beginning of the nineteenth century Hull had around thirty whaling ships, a number which was to increase to fifty-seven in 1815 making Hull by far the biggest whaling port in Britain. Whaling, when successful, was highly profitable but the losses of men and ships was severe, five vessels out of thirty-three being lost in 1808. As the stocks of whales fell and the need for whale oil was replaced by other products, the whaling fleet declined as quickly as it had risen. There were only twenty-seven whaling ships operating out of Hull by 1833 and in 1869 the last Hull whaler, the *Diana* was lost at sea and Hull whaling came to an end.

As the whaling industry declined, the fishing industry grew to become one of Hull's leading employers so that by 1882 it was providing a living for nearly a quarter of the Hull population. The initial fishing smacks found their way to Hull and Grimsby from Brixham and Ramsgate, attracted first to Scarborough, where as late as 1860 as much fish was landed as at Hull, and then to Hull itself where facilities for exploiting the rich North Sea grounds were superior. With access to the growing towns of West Yorkshire and London via the new railways and with fish becoming part of the staple diet for working people, the demand for fish grew so that by 1886 19,000 tons of fish had been landed compared to 1,586 tons in 1854. The fishing boats now worked in fleets and stayed at sea sending fish back to port and being supplied by fast cutters. Ice was brought in from Norway and later manufactured in Hull, to help preserve the catch. Many of the boat owners had worked their way up from deck hands, taking loans to buy their first boat. The trade increased to such an extent that a new dock, the St Andrew's on Hessle Road, was built to house the fleet of fishing boats and was opened in 1883.

All was not well with the industry though and it relied on 'apprentices' to man the boats, many forced to serve or go to prison under harsh laws. Passengers on the New Holland ferry were shocked to see apprentices chained together being sent to the Hedon Road prison for refusing to go to sea. Although this practice was stopped by a new law of 1880, life in the fishing boats remained ten times as dangerous as coal mining and there was a strike by the boat crews in an effort to improve conditions. In March 1883, 180 Hull fishermen were lost in gales and another sixty in 1900. In 1904 the Russian fleet fired on Hull trawlers, thinking they were Japanese torpedo boats, sinking the *Crane* and killing the Captain and a deck hand. Already there were signs that overfishing was happening as catches fell despite the introduction of steam power and trawling nets. There were just a handful of sailing-smacks left in service by the end of the century, the majority of the new steam powered trawlers having been built in Hull. At the outbreak of the first world war, the fishing fleet was pressed into service as minesweepers. Without their services, it would have been impossible for the Grand Fleet to deploy against the German fleet.

For a while steam boats made it possible to travel from Hull to London and Edinburgh and ports in between, in some comfort, rather than take the stage coach but it was the opening of the railway service from Hull to Selby on the 1st of July 1840 which was to prove a turning point in the story of Hull. The first station was in Kingston Street and 4526 passengers were carried in the first week. By 1845 there was a line connecting Hull to Bridlington and in May 1848 Hull's Paragon Station was opened to cope with the increased traffic. In 1854 a line was opened to Withernsea, then a village of 109 people, but soon to be developed as a seaside resort for Hull and ten years later the line to Hornsea was opened. The culmination of Hull's railway building boom came in 1885 with a new line carried through Hull on embankments and linking the coalfields of South Yorkshire with the newly built Alexander Dock in Hull. The net of railway lines stimulated trade and allowed commuters to come into Hull and the townspeople to get to the coast. Ominously, the first petrol powered motor car engines were being developed in the town by Priestmans and although the railways would flourish for another hundred years, the future was with the motor car.

Below
A Steam train pulls out of Paragon Station

HULL IN THE TWENTIETH CENTURY

The brief period from 1901 when Edward VII became king and before the carnage of the First World War, is seen nationally as a 'golden age' and even for a city as relatively poor as Hull, there was a lifting of the spirits.

Hull had achieved City Status in 1897 and a spate of public building began which was to transform the centre of the city which a *Times* writer of 1886 described as consisting of 'small red-brick uninteresting houses'. No respectable person wandered into the city centre and the police patrolled in pairs. The impetus for the transformation was led by Alfred Gelder, many times mayor of Hull and Liberal M.P. for the Brigg division from 1910 to 1918. The Town Hall opened in 1900 followed by the Central Library in Albion Street. In 1901 Jameson Street and King Edward Street were opened and by the outbreak of the first world war, The City Hall, Guildhall, the City Square with its statue of Queen Victoria and splendid public toilets were opened. George Street had been extended to Paragon Square where a statue to the fallen of the Boer War was erected. The King George Dock was opened by the king himself in 1914.

Below
Victoria Square

43

Already by the end of the nineteenth century Hull had public parks where 10,000 people would turn out on a Sunday to hear the band play and the Beverley Road swimming baths was opened in 1905 to join those in Madeley Street and Holderness Road. In 1904 the new Education Committee under the chairmanship of Sir Alfred Gelder took office. Schools were taken out of the hands of the churches and became chargeable to the rates, ensuring adequate funding even if some of the nonconformist clergy went to prison rather than see the church schools benefit from the rates. In 1913 the municipal training college on Cottingham Road opened, to be the forerunner of Hull University.

Below
Pearson Park

Slum clearances began and the largely protestant and teetotal council took the opportunity to reduce the number of public houses from 452 in 1901 to 288 in 1935 by refusing licenses to replace those public houses demolished. Heavy drinking remained a problem and scenes of public drunkenness and rowdiness accompanied many public events, a phenomenon which was to return to the city in the twenty-first century.

There had been horse drawn trams in Hull in the previous century but access to a reliable supply of electricity meant that electric trams could be introduced by the Council in 1899 on Hessle and Anlaby Roads and then in the twentieth century on the other main roads. They were phenomenally popular carrying four million passengers in the first six months and allowing the further spread of housing along the main roads as people were able to use the trams to commute to work and to come into the city centre to shop. The trams continued in service until the late 1930s when they began to be replaced by the new electric trolley buses and petrol buses. Electricity, supplied from the Corporation's plants in Dagger Lane and Sculcoates, was being installed in private homes and was also used to light the streets but this was only partially successful and lamplighters could still be seen lighting the gas lights installed in the last century up until 1939 and gas lights could be found in some minor streets well into the 1960s.

Below
Trams in
Prospect Street

Hull's unique Corporation owned telephone system began in 1903 when the Corporation set up its own exchange in competition with a private company which had been established in 1880. The Hull Telephone Department opened its first exchange at the former Trippett Street Baths in 1904 and by 1906 the Corporation had bought out the private company and was well into profit by 1910. From the beginning, there was pressure from the Post Office to bring the Hull exchange into the National Telephone Company but unlike every other town and city, Hull resisted and to this day maintains its own telephone system with the distinctive cream coloured telephone boxes. The telephone company, known as Kingston Communications from 1987, was always one step ahead of the Post Office, providing lines and calls at cheaper rates and using the phones to relay pop songs and bedtime stories. Kingston's conversion of its network to a digital infrastructure in 1989 was the first all-digital network in the UK. The flotation of the company on the stock exchange in 1999 provided the city with funds to improve the city's infrastructure including the KC Stadium opened in 2002 at a cost of £44 million and now shared by Hull City Football Club and Hull Rugby League Club as well as being a venue for concerts. Hull Kingston Rovers Rugby Club continues to play at their Craven Park ground across the river, where speedway is also an attraction.

Right
Hull's distinctive phone boxes

Rugby and football were always popular in the city and the loud roars from the stadiums at Boothferry Park and Airlie Street rang around the streets on a Saturday afternoon. The two rugby teams were pre-eminent, winning many league titles and cup finals, memorably playing each other in 1980, when the streets of the city were deserted. The football team has never played in the top tier, despite huge support when the team is successful. The problem is one of chronic financial difficulties and attracting the best players to come and live in the city rather than any lack of ambition.

Left
Hull FC v Hull KR

But all was not well in the new city and it could be argued that much public splendour was bought at the price of private squalor. 424 people died from tuberculosis in 1908 alone. Wages for many were still just at subsistence level and unemployment was endemic as the docks were often at the mercy of swings in trade and shortages caused by wars in Europe and America. The bitter dock strikes of the 1890s continued into the twentieth century. The Wilson Shipping Company had been victorious the first time in its conflict with the Dockers' Union, bringing in non-union workers from around the country and using police and troops to get the 'free labourers' to the dock side. But in 1913, a shortage of labour meant that the dockers' demands for increases in pay and shorter working hours were met by the employers. Poor housing and sanitation and air pollution had hardly been tackled before the outbreak of war in 1914 turned attention from domestic to international issues.

All trade with Germany and her allies ended and shipping through Hull fell from 6 million tons in 1913 to 4 million by 1915. In addition a number of Hull ships were sunk at sea. War work in the ship yards and other concerns with government contracts took up some of the slack. The fishing trade was badly hit when the navy commandeered the fishing fleet to be turned into mine sweepers and despite a crash programme of building, numbers did not return to normal until 1915. Most of Hull's many fish and chip shops closed. As in many other British towns and cities the initial enthusiasm for the war meant that thousands volunteered and died on the battlefields of France. Hull lost 7,000 killed and 14,000 disabled. Free school meals were arranged for children who had lost their fathers until the War Office arranged allowances.

For the first time, modern technology brought an overseas war directly to Hull. The city was first bombed by a Zeppelin in June 1915 when 24 people were killed and the raids continued throughout the war until March 1918. Although the primary targets were the docks and shipyards, inaccurate bombing meant that many bombs fell on houses and dozens of civilians were killed. Morale suffered as much as the fabric of the city and there was anger that Zeppelins could hover over the city without being challenged. Only in 1918 did searchlights and fighter planes begin to chase off the bombers.

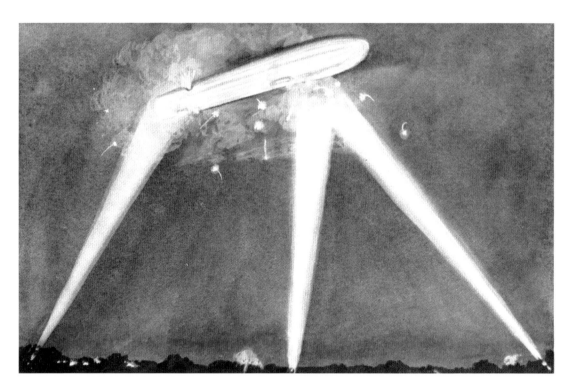

After the war, many parts of the country were gripped by an economic depression which meant mass unemployment and poverty for those out of work. The Hull figures were generally above the national average of 20% of the work force unemployed. Some sectors of the work force were worse off than others and by 1931 half of Hull's 8,500 dockers were without work and the ship yards were badly hit as the demand for new ships virtually ceased. Despite this, Hull still ranked as the third port behind London and Liverpool and for those in work in the engineering firms and mills, the quality of life slowly improved and the birth rate for Hull was above the national average. By 1934 the last of the old earth closets had been replaced by flushing toilets even if it was reckoned by the standards of the 1930s Housing Act that one third of the inhabitants of the city were living in overcrowded conditions.

Above
Zeppelin raids continued on Hull through the First World War

In May 1926, the Trades Union Congress called a General Strike in support of the miners' pay claim and 25,000 Hull workers came out. The government was well prepared and police and armed troops were deployed at the docks to keep food moving. Volunteers, including many undergraduates, were used to keep the trams in service. No deaths were recorded in Hull when the strike came to an end after just nine days but there was much bitterness felt against strike breakers and not every worker got his job back.

The range of entertainment on offer expanded from the theatres, music halls and pubs and clubs to cinema and radio, which were both hugely popular. Hull had thirty cinemas in 1935, attended by 200,000 people every week and seventy-three dance halls. Hull even had its own cinema star, Ronald Colman being born in the city and was proud of Amy Johnson, a Hull girl who achieved international fame with her daring flights around the world in a tiny Gipsy Moth aeroplane. Cycling was naturally popular in such a flat city and the thousands who used their bikes to get to work were joined at the weekends by those who cycled for leisure, being able to quickly reach the surrounding countryside.

Right
Amy Johnson

This steady if uneven improvement in the quality of life was once again interrupted by war. Politics was in the air and Oswald Mosley, Stafford Cripps and Haldane all spoke in the city. Hull's experiences in the 1939 to 1945 war differed in many respects from the 1914 to 1918 war. Although attacked by Zeppelins in the first war, Hull was to suffer much more substantial damage in the second. The docks and factories and the refinery at Salt End were prime targets and Hull was well in range of German bombers once Holland and Belgium had been overrun. Bombing continued throughout the war, the last raid killing thirteen people as they were coming out of the Savoy cinema. 5,000 houses were destroyed and half the central shopping area. In addition, factories, schools and hospitals were hit. There was a similar rush to join the forces but applicants were now more carefully screened and not everyone was accepted. Compared to the losses in action of the first world war, combat losses in the second were comparatively light. Iron railings were removed from houses and the young people of the town were evacuated to safe areas although many of them drifted or were brought back. Trade naturally suffered with the bombing of the docks and the sinking of ships by submarines but the war effort was total and the cost would be counted later.

Below
Hammonds Department store was hit during the bombing of World War II

At the end of the war, reconstruction was the order of the day. The City Council commissioned a development plan from Sir Edward Lutyens and Sir Patrick Abercrombie but it was the city's own development plan of 1956 which was eventually implemented. Temporary prefabricated houses, 'prefabs' relieved some of the immediate housing problems until new tower blocks along the Anlaby Road and a new housing estate at Bransholme to the north of the city provided the much needed housing. The last of the very worst slum housing had gone by 1960.

Right
Tower Block on
Anlaby Road

The docks, the economic powerhouse of the city, had heavy investment, though with hindsight, much of it wasted. The river-side quay, which had been completely destroyed in the war, was rebuilt in 1958 at a cost of £1,750,000. The Victoria Dock was refurbished but proved too small and uneconomic and was filled in. This was the case with all of the docks west of the river which have fallen into disuse. A new dock, the Queen Elizabeth Dock, was opened by the Queen in 1969 and all traffic is now concentrated on the eastern, modern docks.

The fifties and sixties were something of a high point for the city with an economic boom fuelled by the building industry, busy putting up new houses and large department stores such as Hammonds, which had been completely destroyed in the war and the large Co-operative store with its enormous front mosaic. Big money was being made on the trawlers. In the bustle around the city centre, many languages could be heard as the ships' crews came ashore and the old market reverberated with the calls of the stall holders and the smell of frying fish and chips. The Beatles played at the ABC cinema. Hull had its own University since 1954, which drew young people from around the country.

Above
A Hull Trawler
Heads for the Fishing
Grounds

For a time after the war, the fishing industry boomed again with large trawlers working off Iceland to bring home catches of cod, to be gutted and filleted and shipped out by rail by the many Hull fish merchants strung along the Hessle Rd. The end was dramatic. The so called 'cod wars' with Iceland ended in 1976 with Iceland setting up a 200 mile exclusion zone which cut off the rich fishing grounds to English trawlers. With other grounds already over-fished, the number of Hull trawlers able to make a living declined and the once crowded and lively fish dock became virtually empty. One trawler, the *Arctic Corsair*, was saved and is now an exhibit moored outside the Hull Museum. Hundreds of crew and the shore workers who supported them were unemployed at a time when jobs were becoming hard to find in the city.

From 1951 the eleven plus exam was implemented in the city. This allotted children to Secondary, Technical or Grammar schools at the age of eleven according to the results of the exam. Seen by many as divisive, it did allow boys and girls from poorer homes the chance of a good education and many of them became the first in their family histories to go on to University. The system came to an end in the late 1960s with the implementation of the Labour Government's comprehensive schools scheme. They have been less than successful in Hull with the city frequently appearing at the bottom of the national league tables for academic success. In a predominantly working class city, academic success was not necessarily prized as much as a real job on the docks or on a ship or in a factory but these type of unskilled jobs were becoming rarer at the very time when the economy was to falter in the 1970s, throwing many out of work.

Above The last of the eleven plus boys. Riley High School, 1965

Hull's road transport links were dramatically improved with the building of the M62 motorway which linked the city with Leeds, Manchester and Liverpool and the more controversial Humber Bridge which was opened in 1981 and was, at the time, the longest single span bridge in the world. Before the bridge was opened, it was necessary to take one of the paddle steamers from the Riverside Quay to New Holland or drive inland as far as Goole. The new motorway made the round trip much quicker and whether the enormous expenditure on the bridge was warranted by the comparatively light traffic heading into Lincolnshire remains a matter of debate. Nevertheless, the bridge has become something of a symbol for the city. Some cynics have commented that the bridge was meant to make a reality out of the Government's reorganisation of local government in 1974, when the new county of Humberside was created with Hull as the virtual county town. With an eye on population shifts and economic trends, central government casually ignored a thousand years of history and sentiment, abolished the East Riding of Yorkshire and put the north bank of the Humber in with the south bank hoping the two would get along. They didn't and a hasty 'u turn' in 1996 saw the return of the East Riding and Hull once more a unitary authority run by the city council.

Below
The Humber Bridge

Parents rescue their children from Westcott Primary School in the Floods of 2007

The separation of Hull from the old East Riding meant that Hull's performance could be monitored in its own right and the statistics were worrying. Hull's schools were at the bottom of the national league tables and the city council itself was designated the UK's worse performing authority in 2004 and 2005. The local police force also received poor reports and the city's self-confidence took another blow when a Channel 4 TV programme announced that Hull was the worst place to live in the U.K. The city suffered another catastrophe in June 2007 when heavy rain caused widespread flooding in the town, affecting 20% of the city's houses and 90 out of 105 schools. The water quickly receded and so did not provide the dramatic pictures the media could show from Doncaster and Sheffield. Hull felt itself the 'forgotten city' even if it did finally get a visit from the new Prime Minister, Gordon Brown. These figures could well explain the success of the Liberal Party in gaining overall control of the City Council in the 2007 local elections on a programme of reform and redevelopment.

Below
The Pedestrian area

But statistics do not tell the whole story of the city. The visitor to Hull today cannot fail to be impressed by the new developments. 'The Deep' is a state of the art aquarium on the site of the old citadel and the tidal barrier affords protection from rising water for the foreseeable future. The centre has been transformed with a large pedestrianised area and millions are being spent on the St Stephens project. The new £165 million Humber Quays development, now with World Trade Centre status, is adding new high quality office space to Hull's waterfront, including two office buildings and 51 new apartments, a new 200 bedroom 4 star hotel, a restaurant and more high quality office space.

The arts flourish in a city, which nourished Philip Larkin and John Godber prepares to move his Hull Truck Theatre into a new building. The New Theatre provides popular entertainment and the live music scene in Hull has produced bands with a national following. Thousands use the P & O ferries from Hull to Holland for business or leisure and the Hull docks handle 19% of the UK's exports. The city has become a national centre for food processing and new firms are being attracted to the city, encouraged by grants and plentiful labour.

With a population base of 300,000, a world class transport system and a regenerated city centre, confidence in Hull's future is growing.

Philip Larkin

Philip Larkin was born in 1922 and came to Hull in 1955 to be the Librarian at the University. Many of his poems are based on life in Hull, although they have appealed to a world-wide audience. Larkin died in 1985.

That Whitsun, I was late getting away:
Not till about
One-twenty on the sunlit Saturday
Did my three-quarters-empty train pull out,
All windows down, all cushions hot, all sense
Of being in a hurry gone. We ran
Behind the backs of houses, crossed a street
Of blinding windscreens, smelt the fish-dock; thence
The river's level drifting breadth began,
Where sky and Lincolnshire and water meet.

Acknowledgements

The Blackthorn Press acknowledges and thanks the following for their kind assistance in providing photographs and drawings: Hull Daily Mail, Roy Burrell, George Morrow, Alex Avery, Ferens Art Gallery, Hull Museums, Hull Maritime Museum.

The Blackthorn Press has attempted to contact copyright owners of artwork reproduced in this book and it welcomes queries from those not acknowledged above. Queries should be sent to Blackthorn Press, Blackthorn House, Middleton Rd, Pickering YO18 8AL.